Hair of the dog

Food poisoning

Catching some z's

The Emoji-to-English Dictionary

YOUR TEXT-MESSAGE TRAN

LMAO

 adamsmedia

SOL

Published by
Adams Media, a division of F+W Media, Inc.
57 Littlefield Street, Avon, MA 02322. U.S.A.
www.adamsmedia.com

ISBN 10: 1-4405-9140-7
ISBN 13: 978-1-4405-9140-2
eISBN 10: 1-4405-9141-5
eISBN 13: 978-1-4405-9141-9

Printed in China.

10 9 8 7 6 5 4 3 2 1

The emoji phrases found in the book were created by C. Coville. All illustrations in this book were created by Kurt Dolber and were inspired by emojis that were created by various individuals and businesses who hold the copyright to their respective emoji libraries. There was no intent to copy or duplicate any particular type or style of emoji. The sole purpose of the illustrations is to provide the reader with the necessary images to accompany the text of the book.

Many of the designations used by manufacturers and sellers to distinguish their products are claimed as trademarks. Where those designations appear in this book and F+W Media, Inc. was aware of a trademark claim, the designations have been printed with initial capital letters.

Cover design by Frank Rivera.
Cover and interior illustrations by Kurt Dolber.

This book is available at quantity discounts for bulk purchases.
For information, please call 1-800-289-0963.

Contents

Introduction

Let's face it: Texting kind of sucks. There's no easy way to express your tone or your mood, and it's very hard to write "a volcano is exploding outside my window" without using a whole bunch of words. That's why we have emojis: You can just send a picture of a volcano and use the precious time saved to run away from the lava!

Like many great things in the modern world, emojis were brought to us by our friends in Japan. In the late nineties, the cell-phone company NTT DoCoMo sought to attract younger users with fun new text-messaging options. Shigetaka Kurita, one of their designers, ended up developing the emojis we know today. Japanese for "picture character," emojis are a set of encoded pictures that can be easily added to text messages. The idea soon spread outside of Japan, and now users the world over can sprinkle their phone-sex messages with as many eggplants and peaches as they want.

While emojis have made texting easier and way more entertaining than ever before, translating text messages isn't always so simple. Does that little smiling poop mean that your friend likes you, or that he hates your guts? And what on earth does a dancing woman have to do with your best bud's bladder infection? Luckily, *The Emoji-to-English Dictionary* is here to decode it all! With this easy-to-understand guide, you can quickly translate all kinds of emoji combinations into helpful English phrases, and you might even pick up a few new ones to sprinkle throughout your text messages or tweets, too.

So get ready to uncover and use the most helpful—and hilarious—emoji phrases around! After all, using an all-emoji dialect makes us a lot like the ancient Egyptians, and those guys worshiped cats and invented the toothbrush. Who wouldn't want to be like that?

Chapter 1

A Picture's Worth a Couple of Words: Everyday Sayings

What the hell?

GTFO

No shit, Sherlock.

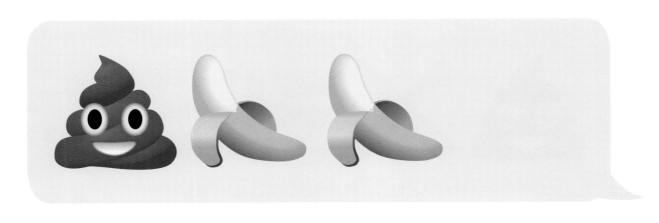

This shit is bananas.

SOL

I can't even.

Best thing since sliced bread

The Emoji-to-English Dictionary

Not my cup of tea

LMAO

Nutcase

Bad hair day

Over the moon

Cool story, bro.

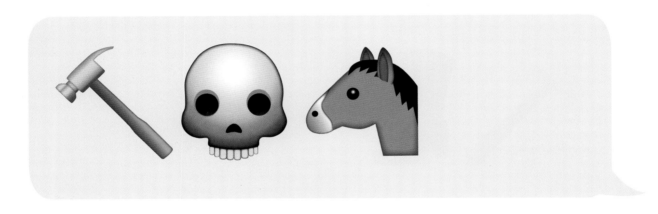

Beating a dead horse

Break a leg!

Chapter 2

Stuff to Put in Facebook Pictures: Hobbies and Food

Vegetarian

Vegan

Cooking for the first time

How old are these leftovers?

Living off ramen

Hungover

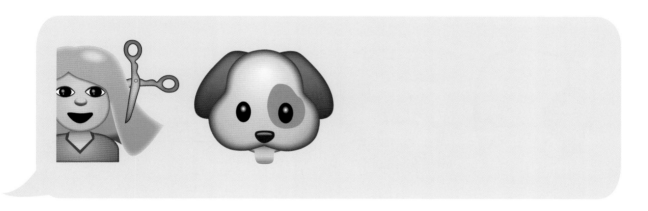

Hair of the dog

Watching cat videos

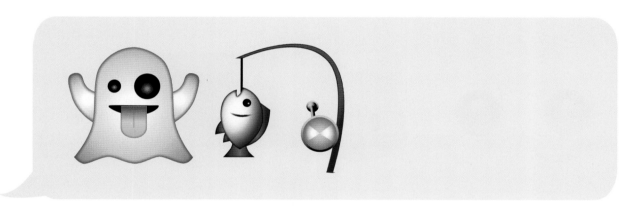

Ghost hunting

Gym rat

Do you even lift?

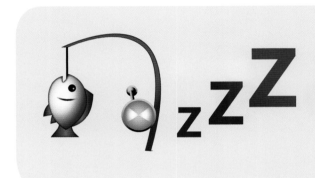

Catching some z's

Dancing like nobody's watching

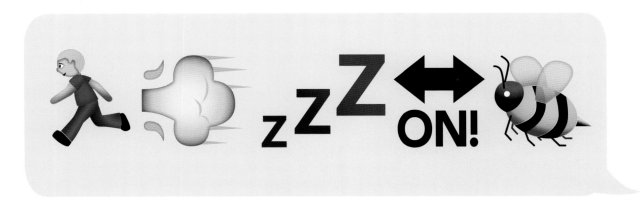

Running like zombies are after me

Chapter 3

Pop Culture, Emojied: Movies and Books

What are you watching?

A Christmas Carol

Independence Day

Planet of the Apes

Blade Runner

Up

Gravity

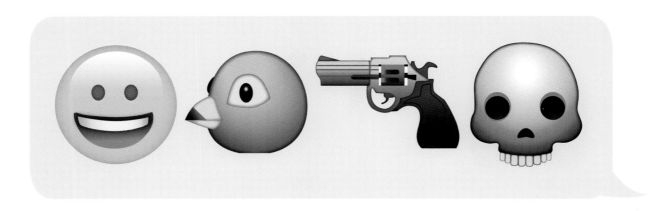

To Kill a Mockingbird

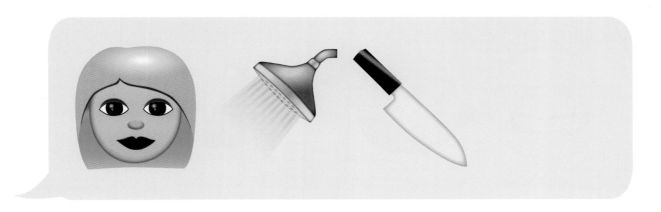

Psycho

Hamlet

Frankenstein

Ghostbusters

Dirty Dancing

Superman

Monty Python and the Holy Grail

Chapter 4

We All Need Someone to Emoji: Sex and Dating

Great in bed

Not great in bed

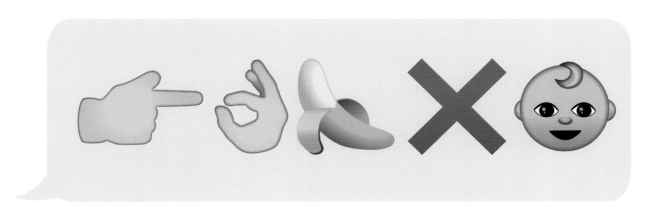

Let's use a condom.

The condom broke!

Baby got back

Let's grow old together.

Mile-high club

OKCupid is full of douchebags.

Up all night to get lucky

The Emoji-to-English Dictionary

Bang me like a screen door!

Hotter than hell

You're a piece of work.

You're my boo.

**Do you want to have pizza and screw? . . .
What, you don't like pizza?**

No dick pics

Chapter 5

Conquer the Office with Emojis: Work

A case of the Mondays

Hump day

Breadwinner

Rat race

Working my ass off

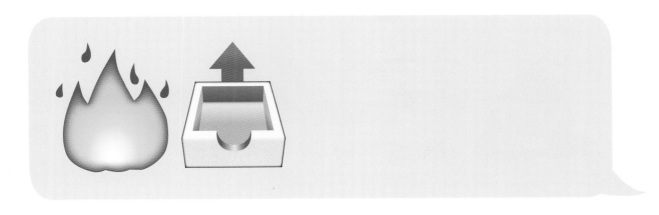

Burned out

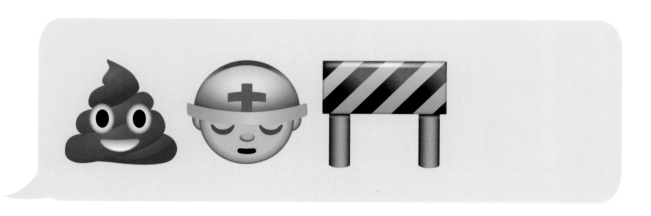

Dirty work

Paycheck

Minimum wage

All work and no play makes Jack a dull boy.

Chapter 6

We're All Going to Die: Health and Medicine

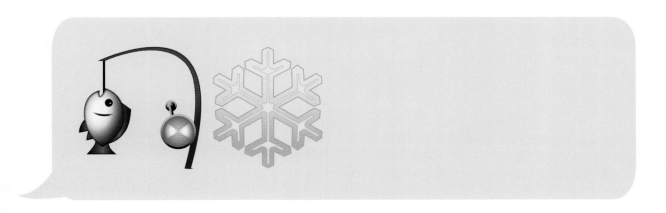

Catching a cold

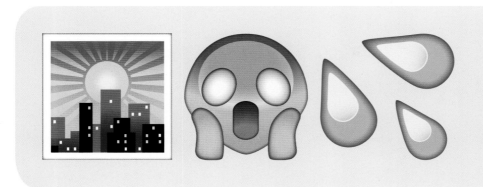

Morning sickness

In labor

C-section or natural birth?

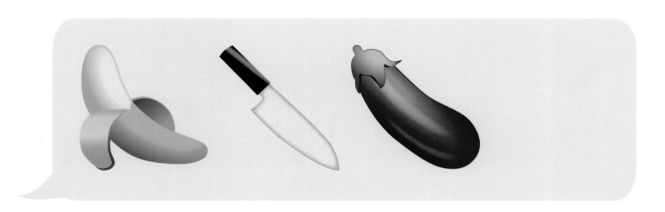

Circumcision

Out cold

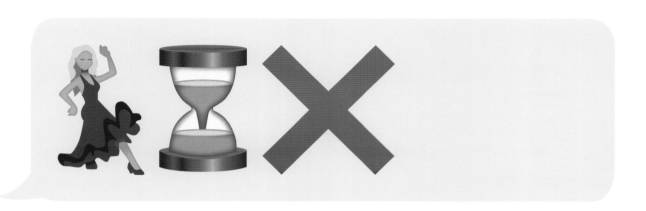

He'll never dance again!

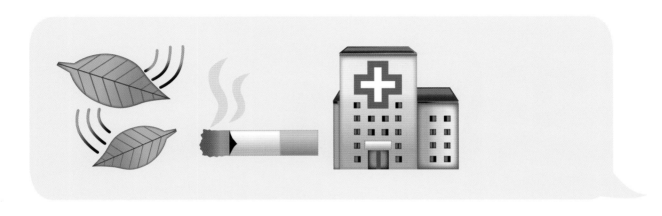

This herb is medicinal.

Food poisoning

Diarrhea

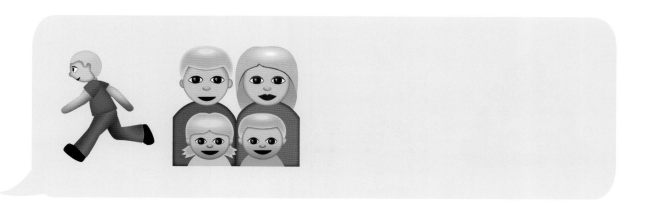

Runs in the family

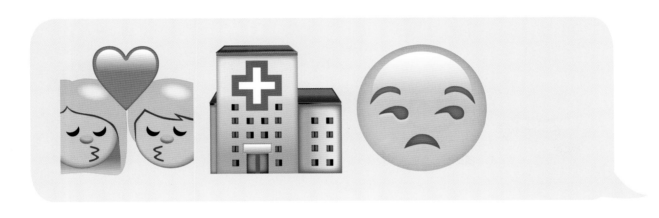

STD

Pain on a scale of 1 to 10

Knocking on heaven's door

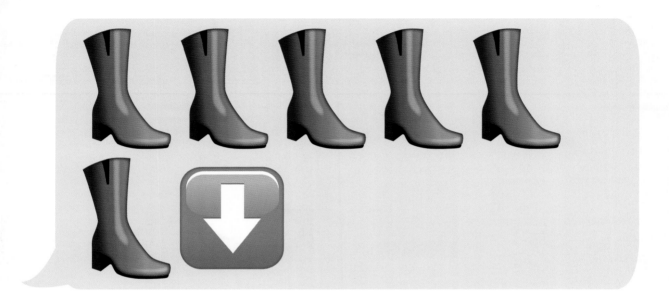

Six feet under

Chapter 7

How to Stop Liking Your Friends: Talking Religion and Politics

Jehovah's Witness

Atheist

Pentecostal

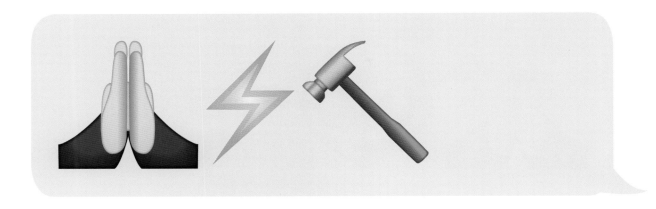

Worshiping Thor

Scientologist

Spiritualist

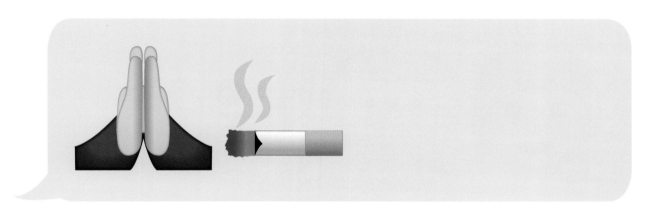

Rastafarian

Theory of evolution

Creationism

A Viking burial

Reincarnation

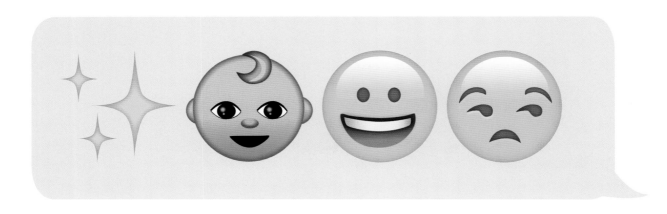

Astrology

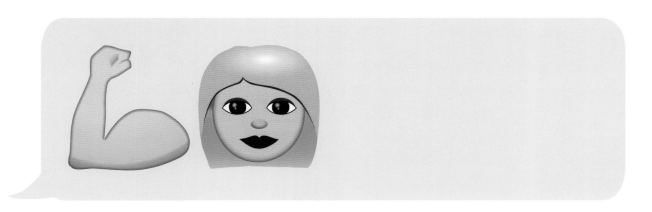

Feminism

Free speech

Death penalty

Chapter 8

Because Everyone Loves Kittens: Discussing Pets and Animals

Clean up after your pet!

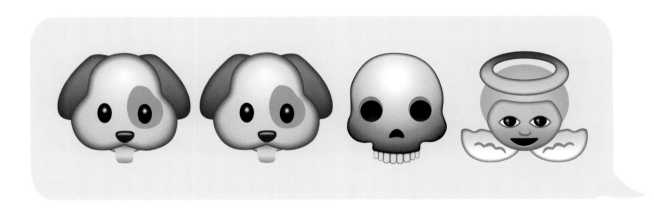

All dogs go to heaven.

A crazy cat lady

Bathing my cat

The dog is marking his territory.

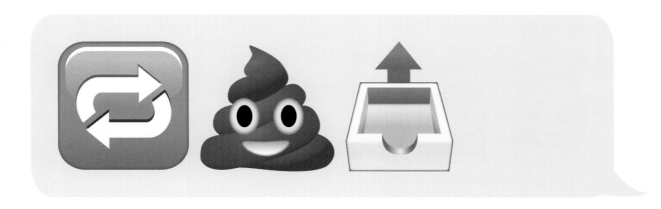

Change the litter box

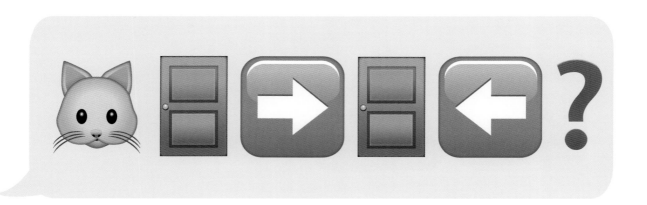

Trying to let the cat out

Not the bees, they're in my eyes!

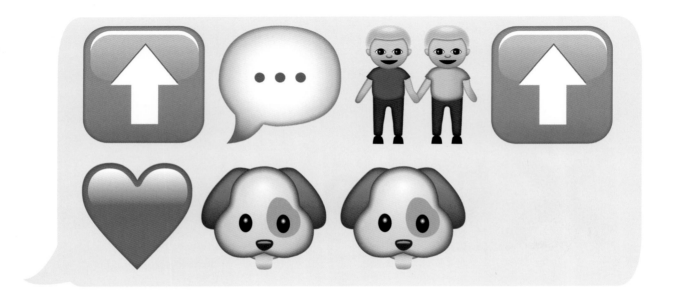

The more I get to know people, the more I love dogs.

Bee sting

Werewolf

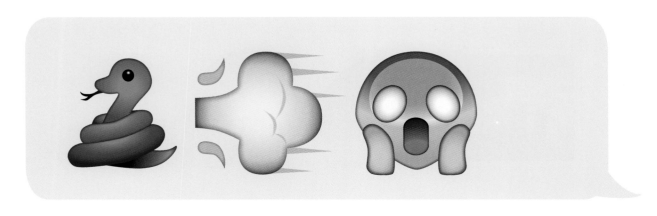

My exotic pet has escaped!

The mob boss left me a message.